Rise Above

For further information and any questions visit our website at www.businessinheels.com; Email: info@businessinheels.com

ISBN: 978-0-6451639-0-2 (paperback)

Typeset by Karinya Kreations, www.kkreations.design

Edited by Steve Sweeney

Compiled, produced, and published by
Business in Heels International Pty Ltd

Contents

———————————

Foreword
by George McEncroe

I am honoured to be invited to write the foreword for this collection. The stories shared within the following pages have been collected by some of the most courageous and clever women in Australia and indeed the world.

As the founder and CEO of a service devoted to the freedom and comfort of women, I look for inspiration regularly amongst my peers. Collections such as this, enable budding innovators to learn and thrive, find comfort and conciliation, as well as humour and templates from which to define a female future.

There were many times as a female Founder that I felt isolated. I had four kids to care for and networking at night or for breakfasts was often just too difficult. It was very hard to hear from women like me, women who had endured difficult separations, financial insecurity and the ongoing economic disadvantage suffered by women who can't or won't pay for child care, unless I downloaded a podcast or read a book.

There exist many seemingly intractable issues facing women in Australia. Women are asked to work for free, we face sexual harassment in the workplace, abuse and violence at home, expensive child care, poverty and homelessness face us when have been separated with the primary care of their children. In the business world, there are very few women to seek guidance from. Creating safe places for women is at the core of my business, and safe places to tell stories is a natural extension of that. Being able to draw on resources like stories here, I hope is enormously helpful to every one who reads this collection.

Shebah was born from collaboration and reimaging the world from a female lens. This collection, rich in diverse stories will help you dear reader, to do the same.

Job title | CEO, Shebah

Sandy *Chong*

Sandy Chong Is a key influence in the Hairdressing Industry. Currently she is the CEO/Director of the Australian Hairdressing Council (AHC) and Director of COSBOA (Council Of Small Business Organisations of Australia) representing small business. She speaks on behalf of the industry to Government, creating relationships to support an industry that is often overlooked.

Her role at the AHC has established better business practices, training and education and building sustainable careers for the future of the industry.

Sandy's vision is to create an industry that has the highest possible standards in ethics, technical ability and workplace practices.

Owner of her own salon Suki for 36 years, Sandy is a business multi award winner as well as being inducted into the Industry's Hall Of Fame. In 2020 Sandy was recognised as one of the country's most influential women by Minister Michaela Cash and Small Business and Family Enterprise Ombudsman, Kate Carnell. She was also the recipient of The Australian Hair Industry Special Recognition Award.

During her career Sandy has written, facilitated and presented business programs nationally and internationally for companies including L'oreal, Redken, Goldwell, Matrix, DeLorenzo, Tigi, GHD, Kerastase as well as the AHC.

Sandy is a respected industry source for the media and has been interviewed as a guest on countless television, radio, press and online platforms.

by Sandy Chong

It's more than keeping up Appearances

The look on her face matched mine. Shock, horror, disbelief. The only difference was she had a bloody nose and I didn't. OMG, did I really do that!?

"May you live in interesting times" is an English translation of a traditional Chinese curse. And, when you're half Chinese and half Irish, well… you can be certain you will always live in interesting times.

My great grandparents, Chee Doc Nomchong (born 1854) and Mary Shem Boo Jung (born 1867) had 15 children and settled in Braidwood NSW from China. Like the other Chinese settlers, they were not popular. However, my great grandparents were especially unpopular because they were wealthy. Back in those days, perhaps to reduce the cultural divide, many Chinese married the Irish and this practice continued for a few generations and explains my heritage.

For all he was a wealthy businessman, Chee Doc struggled to maintain this status as he became bankrupt not once, but twice, and recovered his wealth twice. Shame I didn't inherit any of that wealth, but I do believe I inherited his resilience. My own parents too became bankrupt after owning a

by Sandy Chong

small business in the mining town of Captains Flat. When the mines closed and we lost everything, we moved to a housing commission estate to live in a pale green fibro house. When you're 3, this means nothing until others feel the need to let you know who you are and who you are not… the haves and have nots. Interesting times indeed.

My Irish mother never embraced being married to an ABC (I found out years later this had nothing to do with the national broadcaster. No, it meant Australian Born Chinese.) So in preparation for school, she would painfully curl my hair nightly with rollers, wrap a cotton nappy around my head and send me to bed. She was doing her best to make me look non-Asian and insisted on telling everyone my hair was naturally curly. I looked ridiculous! And even though I was only 4, I knew I looked silly and felt the shame that she felt for my heritage.

Growing up in a Catholic school, with my sister and brother being the only half-casts, allowed me to experience racism and discrimination early in life. When young, you don't know what to do, say or how to stand up for yourself. So for the first 3 years in primary school, I would sit by myself and watch the groups of girls play. I learnt early to like my own company, to not feel lonely and to not feel the need to belong to something or someone that chose to ostracise me. Choose real friends.

Children hurt without realising, often modelling their parents. For me kids would taunt and chant, "Chinese, Japanese, Pekinese, money please." I find it strange that if I tell someone this story today, many still think it's funny. That's very sad for me. I had one particular bully in my state school who would seek me out with her two friends to pick on me after school and threaten to bash my head in. I still remember her name. Patricia was my bully. Once I grew older, I wondered if Patricia had a terrible home life and that was why she picked on others knowing they were weaker than her. I mean… what makes a bully a bully? She never hit me, but I learnt it's not what you do or say, it's how you make a person feel that counts. It may sound odd at this point, but I think that's part of why I gravitated towards hairdressing.

We finally moved from our housing commission house to Sydney and I went to a new high school. How exciting! A new start! It meant new friends who didn't know I'd lived in a fibro commission house. But what you don't confront will always follow you and my new bully was Elouise. She would chant, "Ching Chong Ching Chong," whilst she and her friends threw fruit at me and my friends looked on. So one day, I stood up to her. I took a deep breath and thumped her in the face. The look on her face matched mine. Shock, horror, disbelief. The only difference was she had a bloody nose and I didn't. OMG, did I really do that?

No one bullied me again. I'm not sure this is a lesson to teach or tell, but for me it was a turning point of self-respect. Don't get me wrong, I'm not proud of hitting someone. But I was proud I finally stood up for myself when no one else did. I've always found it hurtful knowing others just watched. To me, those that watch are just as guilty as those that do. Courage is sometimes hard to find but I believe it needs to be in us all.

We may have moved out of the housing estate, but we still had very little money. My cousin and aunt were hairdressers. I thought they were so cool. They wore the latest fashion clothes and makeup and hair.

by Sandy Chong

They looked like they were having the best time ever and I wanted to live like them. So I started to work in salons on a Saturday and Thursday night to earn some pocket money. One of these was the Hair Den in Rozelle. I would arrive on a Saturday at 7am, open the salon, go out the back to a bedroom and wake up the hungover owner, feed his starving dog and cook his breakfast. They say kids today don't have it like we did. Well, maybe that's something we can all be thankful for.

I soon realised there were better salons and headed to the city to a salon called Daisy Bates. I didn't really get an interview. The owner, Leonard Simmons, met me out the front. I told him I wanted to be a hairdresser. He told me I was too short, this would never happen and to not come back.

I went back after a month in the hope he didn't remember me. I was hired on persistence.

Daisy Bates had a vibe I'd never experienced. Hairdressing was a world where there was no judgement. It didn't matter where you were from. The clientele was colourful. The hairdressers were colourful. The salon was exciting, buzzing and I knew I was in the right place. Finally, I found my place… where I belonged. And an industry that did not care about who you were, what you were or where you came from. They didn't care that I didn't have a university degree or whether I had finished school. They lived and worked to make another person feel great about themselves when they looked in the mirror. It made it all worthwhile to see a smiling person. I knew what it felt like to be awkward, to be judged and have zero confidence. Helping others have appearance and confidence transformations all day everyday was what I wanted to do for the rest of my career.

As for being too short...

At the time, the salon was the trendiest in Sydney. So naturally I had to look the part. My first purchase was the highest black and silver, cork wedges I could find. I needed to prove I could be a tall person asap for the boss. I'm not a lover of heights and these shoes confirmed it. One of my most memorable falls was tripping down every stair from the top of a double-decker bus to roll across the bus floor before landing on the street gutter! I have a reputation for excellent face plants and have continued in life to prove this to be true.

I also became known for my trademark makeup. I decided to embrace my Asian background and wore heavy eyeliner to slant my eyes even more. No more pretending to be what I wasn't, who I wasn't.

Oh, and for the record... I was 15 years-old.

Hairdressing for me was something I lived for. I don't really feel I had any special technical talent. But I understood how we all have the ability to put a smile on someone's face, make them feel special, respected and appreciated. I was a great listener and committed to learn something from every person I met, no matter their age or gender. I wanted them to feel, no matter what was happening in their life, a visit to our salon was an escape from their reality and a time to be just who they want to be without judgement. I've shed many tears with my clients and many belly laughs too. The relationship between a hairdresser and client can grow to something unique, somewhere between friend and family. I think I've seen and heard it all in a lifetime of clients. I didn't need to read storybooks because I would hear the highs and lows of hundreds of life stories and real-life dramas every day. Reality TV comes nowhere near the day-to-day insights of a hairdressing salon!

I only have great memories of my apprenticeship and hope that for my own apprentices over the years I've been able to create a culture that will leave them with happy and wonderful memories of their time with me. I know there are many in our industry who are committed to this too, and if the business you work in doesn't have your best interests at heart then find another business. I have always managed my employees with three life rules.

- The more effort you put in, the more you get back.
- Know what you know and know what you don't know.
- Never stop learning.

I opened my business, Suki, 35 years ago. I started with just 3 staff and within 12 weeks I had grown to 9 staff. We were the new business in town and everyone wanted a booking. As a business owner, I had no idea what I was doing. I felt overwhelmed and out of control. Ever felt like this? I had to step up fast or fail fast. In those days, there were no coaches or mentors so I'm going to be honest... I winged it! I made lots of business mistakes, learnt fast and moved on.

I was committed to training and upskilling and was invited to become a part of a group for Redken which involved presenting business and life skills to salons. They taught us presentation skills, acting and how to be happy with yourself. I remember dancing wildly in a training session, something you would never see me do! I was the wallflower after all. This was a massive learning curve for me and one of great growth. It was the 80s and much of what was covered in our sessions was mental health, financial independence, confidence and being successful.

While still running my own business, I became a regular business speaker on the national circuit in NZ, Singapore, Hong Kong and many offshore conferences. I wrote workshops on business, staff management and how to develop a loyal, productive business culture for your staff. My own salon was awarded 5 times in the national industry business awards and I was endorsed into the Hall of Fame in 2013 and awarded a special recognition Award in 2020 for my services to the Industry. My existence in the industry has never been to win awards, however the recognition makes you a negotiable product.

After winning one of these awards, someone congratulated me saying it was good that an underdog won.

I went home and looked up underdog.

Fast forward to my current position, CEO of the Australian Hairdressing Council (AHC.) Here, I'm representing the industry I love to politicians and others. Honestly, some days I feel like I'm back in kindergarten and playing by schoolyard rules. You see, lobbying is a new playground for academics and how much more out of my comfort zone could I be? When I mention hairdressing, I can see their faces immediately change and I know they're thinking I'm frivolous and not worthy of respect. Really, I'm under more pressure to prove my advocacy is worth listening to than to sustain meaningful arguments. Good thing I looked up underdog all those years ago. However, I will continue to advocate for an industry the Government often takes for granted.

One thing I do know is small business and small businesspeople. They work hard. They work long hours. They are often working for their staff. They don't sleep well. They take risks that can make or break them.

by Sandy Chong

The AHC joined the Council of Small Business Organisations of Australia (COSBOA) and I found another community who stand up for small business rights. I found people who stand up for me.

It's taken my lifetime so far to accept there will always be bullies, there will always be racists. There are some who will never get you, never like you, never accept you, never listen to you.

Then there are those that just see you for who you are, another human who arrived with nothing and will leave with nothing regardless of gender, race, wealth or knowledge. To me they are the rich ones, the smart ones, the ones who are my mentors, my family, my friends. They are kind to all kinds. They are all success stories.

Despite their earlier treatment of me, I hope my bullies became their own heroines and made a positive difference in others' lives. If they'd come into my salon, I'd have done my best to give them the confidence to achieve this.

Heather *Kennedy*

Life is a challenge, an array of new things to explore, overcome and conquer. And that is why, life is great…

Unlike many of our species I love change. When something new comes up I relish it. To do the same thing day in day out is not for me. The thrill of learning and implementing new things is what makes me thrive. I think that is why I have loved all my time working in my business, K.I.S. Accounting & Bookkeeping Professionals, that I founded in 1999 working with over 1000 businesses and satisfying their uniquely different needs.

I am not one to accept that something can't be done if I want it enough. This mindset has given rise to many adventures that my two children and I would never have had if I'd listened to the people that told me "You can't do that". In my story you will read of our trip to England which we did on a beyond hair string budget. My friends and family thought I was crazy but we had a fantastic time that we still re-live to this day. When everyone said I was mad to buy a 1/600th share in a farm at the Western foot of the Blue Mountains, I didn't listen either, and for over 25 years my family and I have spent weekends (and School Holiday weeks) riding horses and Trail bikes, swimming and socialising around a Fire Pit, while making many life-long friendships, and all on a budget of a Single Mum.

Being a Single mum and a want-to-be Entrepreneur wasn't always holidaying and fire-pits though. I experienced all the juggling, frustration, exhaustion and moments of both joy and guilt that many of you would be aware comes as part and parcel of being a mum running a business. It was hard work and so many times I wanted to give it all up, but unfortunately (or fortunately) "Give up" is also not part of my vocabulary. So I plodded on and tried to be the best mum I could be while also trying to give my all to my clients.

My children are now grown up and I have some new roles alongside that of business owner; Carer to my mum who lives with us; and Director of three local Charities. I am also starting to explore my other passion, which is writing and hope that this Chapter will be the start of many more chapters to come...

Title	Founder and manager of K.I.S. Accounting & Bookkeeping Professionals
Website	www.kisaccounting.com.au
Twitter	http://twitter.com/kisaccounting1 (@kisaccounting1)
K.I.S. Facebook	www.facebook.com/kisaccounting
Personal Facebook	www.facebook.com/heather.kennedy.5070
LinkedIn	www.linkedin.com/pub/heather-kennedy/1/175/575

by Heather Kennedy

Rainy days and Mondays

I reached out as slowly as I could for my mobile phone that lay in the centre console of my car. Trying hard not to show any movement, I barely breathed. I popped my head under my sleeping bag, drew the phone to me and dialled 999.

"Police," I whispered. "I think there may be a robbery going on at the Petrol Station I'm at with my children."

It was 24 May 2002, and I along with my two children, Chantelle (then 12) and Tim (11), were on the adventure of a lifetime travelling through England in a hired Ford Focus. I was 32, a single mum and a budding entrepreneur with a two-and-a-half-year-old business.

The fact that I had no money to travel was just the next obstacle, not an insurmountable barrier, yet it was one of the reasons for my current predicament which found Chantelle, Tim and I tucked up (the kids asleep, me still awake) in our Ford Focus outside a carwash in a petrol station somewhere in England. And when I say 'somewhere' that is pretty much what I told the English police during my 999 call.

"Where are you?" the Policeman asked.

by Heather Kennedy

"I'm in a petrol station," I answered in a whisper. "I'm not exactly sure where it is but it's near a big roundabout."

"I'll need more than that," he said patiently.

"Ok, well I was at Streatham Ice and Leisure Centre, celebrating my son's 11th birthday, and we drove about 2 hours from there heading towards Shoreham. I was on the main road when I had to pull over because I was too tired to drive safely and I came to a huge roundabout and now I'm at the petrol station just past the off ramp."

When we first arrived at the petrol station, I got permission from the manager to park next to the carwash and the kids had gone to sleep in their sleeping bags in the back of the car. About an hour later, two cars and some motorbikes turned up revving their engines. A group of people had jumped out of the car, gone into the shop and a lot of yelling had ensued. I had crept lower in the front seat while wrapped in my own sleeping bag. When they still hadn't left after ten minutes and the cars still had their engines running and the yelling was continuing from inside the shop, I had finally dared to move enough to pick up my mobile phone and make my whispered call.

Somehow, despite my vague attempts at informing them of our location, the police worked out our whereabouts and sent some patrol cars. When they arrived, I decided it was best to get the heck outta there. Still in my sleeping bag, I turned on the car, hit the accelerator and drove as fast as I could away from the scene. When the adrenalin slowed, I pulled over got out of my sleeping bag and fastened the children's seatbelts. And yes, it is possible to drive an automatic car in a sleeping bag!

That was just one of the many (mis)adventures we had on our 6-week trip. Did I plan our holiday? No… other than the essentials. I was too busy finishing client work, training new contractors, oh and we moved to a new house the day before we left for England (I won't do that again – my poor friends and the removalists just about had to pry me out of chair and away from my computer so they could move the last things left in the house.)

We arrived at Sydney Airport, Chantelle and Tim brimming with excitement and me nearly breaking down from exhaustion. I hadn't gone to bed at all the night before and was still doing the final packing when the airport bus came to pick us up. I desperately needed a coffee but unfortunately my budget (or lack of it) didn't allow for that. My next client payment was not due for a couple of days and until then we had literally nothing in the bank. I wasn't too concerned as our first few night's accommodation in London had been pre-paid and my client payments would arrive in time for us to have a bit of fun.

Our first snag occurred on day four when we left London to head for the country. With my 12-year-old daughter the official navigator of the trip, it took us about 6 drive-bys of Buckingham Palace to leave London and head out of the city. (I know that sounds like the Griswold's from National Lampoon, but it really did happen…)

With no accommodation booked after those first few days in London, it was time to find somewhere to stay for the night. It turned out that camping sites were not as easy to find as I had hoped so we didn't arrive at our first campsite until 11.00pm. The campsite managers were a little surprised to see us at that time, but luckily for us, they let us in. Unluckily, however, by that time Tim (the experienced camper of the three of us) was fast asleep. And he is not someone you want to wake once he's asleep. That left Chantelle and I to work out how to put up our tent in the dark at the beginning of a rain shower.

Forty-five minutes later, the tent was up. Then we hit our next snag. The raised camp-bed I had purchased for myself was about thirty centimetres longer than the tent. We solved that by putting it diagonally across the centre of the tent and out the front door. Then we squeezed Chantelle and Tim's blow-up mattresses on either side before snuggling up for a well-deserved night's sleep.

Then came snag number 3. We woke up in the morning to discover our $50 Reject Shop tent (never opened and tested) was not waterproof and with the door of the tent partially open to fit my camp-bed, even less so! We weren't just wet… we were drenched to the skin!! Our pillows and sleeping bags had to be wrung out and Chantelle and Tim, whose blow-up beds were lower than mine, were literally floating in a pool of water. Nevertheless, we had had a good night's sleep, oblivious to it all until we woke up. Thankfully, it was summer, so we were warm… and wet.

Another memorable night of our holiday was the night we stayed at Cousin David's house. He didn't have a spare room so we slept in his loungeroom with Chantelle and Tim on their blow-up mattresses and me in his recliner chair. When we arrived at the house, I had commented on some of the antiques he had in his lounge room including an antique fireplace mantel that contained lion faces that were over 1000 years old and a beautiful antique lamp. Somehow, in the middle of the night, I managed to tip the recliner in my sleep and woke up upside down about to knock over his antique lamp, which I miraculously grabbed. It then took me several minutes to wake up one of my children to rescue the lamp and tip me back upright again!

We had so many adventures on our six-week holiday driving all the way to the bottom of Britain (Land's End) right up to the very top (John 'O'Groats in Scotland.) We slept in our tent, in the car a few more times, at relatives' houses and in bed and breakfasts when the budget allowed. And we even managed two days in Paris, although that was cut a bit short by missing our plane and having to catch a later one. Have you ever explored the Louvre in an hour? We did by literally running the whole way around!

The worst day of every week on our holiday (and the day I came to dread!) was Monday. Why? Well, I had decided (in my wisdom?) that I wouldn't hand over all client work to my new staff as I could manage it while I was travelling. (I needed the money and we can work from anywhere, right? Wrong!)

It may have been all right if I could fast forward to 2021 technology. However in 2002, with dial-up internet which I had to run through my Siemen's mobile phone… well, let's just say it was a nightmare every week. You see, phones and laptops need electricity. Though often taken for granted, when sleeping in cars and tents, this basic commodity was hard to come by.

So Mondays became our nightmare day. You see Monday was the day I had to run a payroll for over fifty security guards. The timesheets were emailed to me each Monday morning and it took over four hours to download them via the mobile on a dial-up connection. So every Monday, I had to find somewhere with electricity to plonk my very patient children and myself for over six hours to download and prepare the payroll. (The only internet cafés they had at that time were in the major cities, where mostly we were not.) On the good days we would be at a relative's house or at a bed and breakfast. Although I can't say my relatives were too thrilled about it as it rather interrupted their plans for the few days we had together. Regardless, at least we were comfortable and had a stable source of electricity.

However, it turned out those Mondays were easy compared to the ones spent in a tent or the car. You see, I had expected the camp sites to have big recreation rooms with power points, like most in Australia. Not so in England.

So we ended up in the strangest of places sometimes...

Once we were in a room full of brochures that was about 3m x 2m for our 6-hour stint. The brochure room had one advantage – brochures! Not only did they help keep the kids entertained, but I was also able to find an Indian restaurant that did tent delivery! They delivered our dinner to our brochure room and I got a beer delivered too. I will never forget the look of horror on the campsite manager's face when she came in and found us having Indian (which she said was "awful smelly stuff") in her brochure room. Luckily, her husband took pity on us and let us stay until my payroll was done.

All the way through that episode I was certain of one thing… those security guards were going to get paid!

So why am I telling this story? It's just one of many times through the life of my business where I have had to juggle the demands of business (trying to keep clients happy and keeping enough money in our pockets) with the demands of motherhood. Having read my story so far, you're probably thinking I am crazy. (I know my relatives and friends thought so.) But at the end of the day, I did what I had to do to be a good business owner, the mostly sole provider to my children and give my kids and I many memorable experiences. Chantelle and Tim are 30 and 31 now and have so many crazy and wonderful memories of that holiday.

When I first started my bookkeeping and accounting business on 19 November 1999, I was 30 and Chantelle and Tim were 10 and 9 respectively. I started the business so I could have freedom around the children. I wanted to be that mum who went to all their school and social events, went to P&C meetings, volunteered for the canteen, and did my dance and soccer mum duties. I did most of those things (though the canteen and P&C didn't last long) but in hindsight, the freedom the business bought me was highly debateable. I could swing my hours to do quite a bit with the children, but that just meant having to work every other available second, including long into the night. And every so often something had to give.

During that start-up phase, I was still studying at university (I had already completed my accounting qualifications at TAFE in 1997 and wanted to add a university degree to my qualifications.) In the end, I had to give up the study (late in 2002) as I was already putting about 100 hours per week into my new and growing business. With the kids, the business and study, well... it was just too much. My body literally just could not take it. I had no choice and stopped with only five subjects left.

As difficult as that was, I will never forget my extremely 'proud mama' moment watching my

by Heather Kennedy

daughter graduate from university less than ten years later. I didn't get to wear the gown and get the photo and the certificate, but I felt just as proud (if not more) watching her.

My business has had many highs and lows over its life so far. I am immensely proud to have been able to provide a very flexible working environment for my staff, many of whom were or still are mum's just like me. Many of my wonderful staff are now great friends. One person who I could not have lived without was Megan. She worked for me for over 10 years while my children were growing up. She cooked and cleaned and took Chantelle and Tim to many of their after-school activities. She was my lifeline that I could not have done without. She is still one of my best friends and I will be forever grateful. And who could have known when I took on my two youngest employees, Rabia and Vesper, (both just 19-years-old when they started) how amazing they were going to be. They are both still with me and Rabia, now in her 30's, is a mum too and has brought her two gorgeous and very well-behaved boys into the office many times during the school holidays.

One of my big high's was in 2014 when I purchased (with help from the bank) my first house. Until then, we had always rented. To build and own my own home was an amazing feeling. To put the icing on the cake, Tim landscaped the whole house with the help of a couple of friends. Now I have my very own Bali paradise. Not only is it beautiful, but every time I look at it, I am filled with such pride that it was made by my son's own hands.

Being a mum and owning a business was never going to be easy. If I knew then what I know now, I am not sure I would have ever taken the first step. The hardest thing of all was the feeling of guilt that you are not giving your children all they need. I really struggled to find the time to do things like help them with their homework or just sit and talk on a day-to-day basis. Conversely, they struggled with my near permanent connection to the phone and the computer. It often felt to them like the business was more important than they were. This caused a lot of frustration and tears for all. Though my business was flexible, I think a regular 9-5 job would probably have ultimately given me more time with them growing up. By the time I realised that, my business had become bigger than just me. And let's call a spade a spade… it brought me a huge amount of satisfaction.

My journey is not over. My children have grown up and my business has too, (turning 21 last year!) I now have this thing called a weekend which I haven't quite worked out what to do with yet. My business is still growing and I am also director of three charities. But now I've reached 50 and I have decided it's time to tick off some of my Bucket List items. Writing books is one of those and this is the beginning of that journey for me. I have weathered the path of juggling a business with motherhood and survived. I have two fantastic adult children, a great business and my own beautiful home to show for it.

Was it easy? No.

Was it worth it? Yes.

Life is good!

_____

Jo *Cavanagh*

I believe passionately that every child's birthright is to be loved and nurtured for all aspects of their development. Through my story, I am hoping to share the origins and life empowering consequences of that belief.

In 2021, emerging from the 2020 pandemic lock down in Melbourne, I am cherishing my abundance which has been challenged by forced family separations and anxieties for each other. This highlights what we value and has led me to look back on who and what has shaped my understanding of family, parenting and community. I reflected on how the personal became professional and now personal again.

My husband Robert and I have just celebrated our 49th wedding anniversary and life together with four wonderful children, partners and four grandchildren (so far!). In 1972 we could never have imagined our family and so many wonderful life experiences. We were young. We were in love but scared. We had found refuge in each other.

In deciding what to share, just as me, I have reconnected with my inner child, reassuring her she was as innocent as any other child and family problems were not her fault. Sure, she would make mistakes, but all would be well and she would do well. This has been a self nurturing process as a woman, as a mother and a grandmother. Having stepped down from my executive career in 2020 I was looking to find just me, and writing with an open vulnerable heart is part of this process. I hope this intention will resonate with our readers.

Twitter | @JoCavanaghAU
LinkedIn | Jo Cavanagh OAM CF MAICD
Website | www.jocavanagh.com

by Jo Cavanagh

Back at the Beginning

When I close my eyes, I can see Jackie sitting in front of me. She's crumpled over, hugging herself, speaking in whispers.

She was one of many children who had chosen to trust me as their social worker; to share what was happening to them. My heart would thump in my chest and ache for their pain. My mind would race as I listened, gently probed with questions and tried to provide reassurance. In the 1970's and 80's, no one talked about the abuse of children living in residential care and, in general, most did not believe it happened.

Jackie told me her "cottage father" was coming into her bedroom at night and into her bed. She was scared of what would happen. "I don't want you to say anything," she told me. "He says it's our secret and bad things will happen if I tell. He says I come to you because you're special but if you tell, everyone will know you're bad. No one will believe you and they'll all say you're just a troublemaker." Jackie was 12 when this started and 13 when she told me. For a whole year she had carried this burden alone, fearing it was her fault because she was bad and unlovable. She believed not even her parents could love her which was why they had abandoned her to state guardianship and care. Her mother was frequently hospitalised with a serious mental illness and her father was unknown. No family had been found who could care for her. She was not to blame for being in care.

I started hearing these stories in 1976 when I first worked at a youth training centre for girls who were described under the law at the time as "exposed to moral danger." Together in a lock-up institution, we had girls abused by parents, girls sexually abused by men, girls who were unsupervised and on the streets at night and girls who had committed assaults and burglaries. Whilst there were many wonderful carers who did their best to comfort and look after them, some didn't. In the absence of training and detailed standards of care, many were worse off as a result of coming into care. I desperately wanted to change this. But could one person make a difference? Could an individual social worker have the power to change what was too confronting for most people to even want to know?

Jackie became a turning point for me. I felt so helpless to protect her and heal her pain. At the time under these circumstances, the system determined children be removed from the care home whilst the carers stayed on pending an investigation by the employer. So Jackie was moved yet again. This time, however, she was separated from her sisters and brother. It truly was a nightmare for her. As a social worker, I was part of the system and part of the problem. I was doing my best but knew it was nowhere near good enough.

When I was trying to help Jackie, I was also a mother myself with two children with my loving husband, Robert. We had met as teenagers and married young. We had both benefited from free and supported university education, had secure employment and a mortgage. But my life hadn't always been that good. I felt Jackie's pain of the rejected child. In fact, it was my own childhood which fuelled my drive to help vulnerable children.

I look back on the lives of my own parents with sadness. My father had demobbed in Australia after serving in the British Navy during World War 2. My mother sailed out from London to join him and they married in Melbourne with no family members present. They went to live in the back blocks of suburbia with dirt roads and an outside dunny. I don't think this was quite the life my mother expected and perhaps she was unwell after my birth. However, even as an adult, I never really learned the truth about what led to me spending significant periods of my childhood living with other people, including my maternal grandmother when she migrated later.

In the late 50's and 60's, my mother developed her talents with roles on radio, television and as a compare for department store fashion parades. I felt I became visible to her when I was useful as a child model, but only whilst on stage. My memories are of being abandoned to the care of strangers when the show was over. This included during tours around regional centres in Victoria. Any protests from me were not tolerated. I learnt to hold my fears inside rather than be on the receiving end of her anger. These were times of great loneliness, anxiety and feeling unsafe – all emotions I recognised in children like Jackie who needed an adult to make them feel safe and loved.

Through my teen years, my relationship with my mother continued to deteriorate. For days she would not speak to me. She would glare at me then look away when I entered a room. I would feel invisible and did not understand why I caused her so much anger. I had a younger brother, born when I was 11, whom I adored and loved looking after. However, there were many health issues and periods of hospitalisation for both him and my mother which were not explained. My father, whom I still believe was a gentle man at heart, seemed to increasingly withdraw into his own world and exempt himself from parenting. This was preferable to the fights of earlier years, but the anger was always there, simmering under the surface of so many conversations which did and did not happen. My memories are of constantly feeling I was walking on eggshells, waiting for the next explosion about something. And that something often seemed to be about me so I would feel it was my fault.

It's not surprising that school and my friends became really important to me. I was so fortunate that in better times I had been sent to a private girls' school where the teachers were just wonderful. As our family situation deteriorated, they seemed to gather me in. A scholarship allowed me to continue on and complete to Year 12 and achieve my preferred place at university.

By 1971, Robert had been my boyfriend for a few years and he gently encouraged me to seek help at a local family counselling service. It was my last year of school. I was depressed about my home situation and in a constant state of anxiety. I look back and wonder what difference it would have made if my parents had been able to seek help with me. But they would never have even entertained the idea! Their very English upbringings necessitated keeping quiet and pretending everything was fine.

The culmination of my life at home with my parents was as innocent as being late home from attending a local conservation protest to save trees. This led to a final violent scene and I left, unable to return. I was 17 and just knew I could not cope with the anxiety, anger and walking on eggshells any longer. My teachers supported me and found me a place to stay with a local family: a family I had not known before, and whose kindness I will never forget.

I was scared and Robert was my refuge. We married early the next year and commenced an amazing life together. After completing my Bachelor of Arts, I went on to complete a Bachelor of Social Work with honours and started working to help improve the lives of vulnerable children. After 7 years, the urge to have children overwhelmed my fear of being a mother and we started our family.

Around the time I met Jackie, I had discovered the work of researchers in the United States and Canada about the abuse of children in out of home care. This research fed my determination to do more; to raise awareness that we were failing these vulnerable children who needed to be heard and believed. By chance, I saw a small advertisement in the weekend paper. It invited applications to the Churchill Memorial Trust for a fellowship to support overseas study and bring back knowledge to advance your chosen professional discipline in Australia. My inadequate attempts to help Jackie inspired my application.

So, bearing in mind where I'd come from, just imagine how amazed I felt when I found myself in front of interview panels, next being selected, then invited to Government House in Victoria to receive one of those coveted fellowship awards. I remember stepping out into the ballroom and turning heads. The collective intake of breath around the room seemed quite loud! You see, by then I was 8 months pregnant with our fourth child, and pregnant women with careers were still an unexpected, and not necessarily socially approved, novelty.

The Governor's wife, Jean McCaughey, assisted with presenting the awards. She was a social worker and social justice campaigner. She warmly greeted me and leant forward to ask quietly, "You will go, won't you?"

"Yes," I said. "We are all going. My husband, our three children and the new baby. Somehow we are going to make it happen." "Brilliant," she said. "Let me know how you get on."

And make it happen we did. Relying on new-fangled fax machines and international phone calls, I connected with researchers and planned our 3-month trip around the US and Canada. Robert's accounting skills were invaluable to develop our 10-page spread sheet with all details of flights, accommodation, costs and payments, contacts and professional visits. A few friends tried to talk us out of travelling with our children, particularly as neither of us had ever been overseas. Yet with Sam 11, Katy 8, Lucy 2 and Abi at 6 months, well… we knew we'd make it work. We had hoped to travel and return before Abi was crawling. With all the extra hands-on care and time together, you could just see Abi growing and developing as we travelled. She was standing up in the sky cot on the plane on the way home! I had the most amazing learning experience and we had an extraordinary family adventure together. We had cashed in insurance policies and superannuation to fund the trip and it was worth every cent.

On my return, I had research data, practice and systems reform recommendations to share. The most significant finding was that children were 7 times more likely to experience abuse as a result of being placed in substitute care. The key experts I had consulted all predicted that, once the significance of this issue was recognised in Australia, we would begin to hear about problems in all settings where the vulnerabilities of children could be exploited. This included schools, sports clubs, scouts and community groups. This was 1990. It would be over a decade until we had a national inquiry into "Children in Institutional Care" in 2003, and the Forgotten Australian's apology in 2009. In 1990, I provided my report and shared findings and recommendations as widely as I could through conference presentations and publications. The Victorian Government Department of Community Services contracted me to develop with them the first standards for out of home care, discipline policies to guide carers in the management of children's behaviour, to document the rights of children in care and complaints processes for children to report mistreatment by carers. From 1990 to 1995 I worked as an independent consultant for the government and many care agencies around Victoria. The information and program resources I had to share were embraced by managers and practitioners. Our Community Services sector was keen to understand how we could do better and improve lives for children in care. My program of work went on to include research on the educational needs of children in care, reforms to strengthen collaboration between the care and education systems, and the development of alternative dispute processes in the Children's Court.

I am so proud to say, this determined, individual social worker, played a part in all of this and the consequent improvement of children's lives.

Throughout this time though, I remained troubled by the possibility that we could do more to stop the need for children to be removed from families and placed in care. When financial stress, poverty and mental illness, drug and alcohol abuse and family violence come together in a family, the complexity of problems get in the way of parenting and looking after children. It seemed to me that it was still a better option, whenever it would be best for the child, to improve the ability of parents to look after their children than remove them. So my next career chapter, as a CEO of a family service organisation, commenced in 1995. It focussed on improving services for vulnerable families and preventing the need to remove children whenever possible. Poetically, this was at the very agency which had helped me, as a teenager, in 1971.

There have been many other opportunities along the way to serve the community in leadership and advisory roles at regional, state, national and international levels. My belief that every child has a birth right to safety and loving care has driven me professionally and personally. As a mother of four, and now also a grandmother of four, and with an enduring, loving marriage of 49 years, I know I am incredibly fortunate. People have been generous to me at critical times and this has given me confidence to develop and use my abilities. I am living proof that childhood trauma does not have to define a life. When other caring adults with goodwill and skills are backed by a society that cares, children who have been harmed can recover and in turn contribute to that society. The value is multiplied and returned many times over.

I have also always believed that we can do better and am reluctant to settle for less than the best. We all deserve justice and fairness; none more so than vulnerable children. Because of this belief, I know at times some have found me challenging. One male CEO told me in no uncertain terms that I was "a difficult woman." At the time I felt reduced and disempowered. The feeling that I was a cause of problems and less than worthy has stayed with me over the years. That was my childhood legacy. Later though, I wondered what my gender had to do with the situation. Reflecting back, I realise now how many times my self-doubt was triggered by gender discrimination. Whilst Helen Reddy inspired me in the 70's with "I am strong, I am invincible..." so many times I have felt less than...

In 2014 however, I had the most exhilarating and rewarding experience of my career. Members of my team at work nominated me for the AFR 100 Women of Influence Award. We were advised to attend the presentation ceremony at the Sydney Town Hall and I travelled there with my husband and small group of key supporters. The Not for Profit and Social Entrepreneurship category was the last of 10 award groups to be announced. When the winner was announced as Jo Cavanagh, it took a few moments to realise that was me! I went up onto the stage and from the podium looked out at this most amazing scene of lights and 1,000 guests, mostly women. They were all applauding; they were all applauding me. I was absolutely overwhelmed. This room was filled with extraordinary women who were successful across all disciplines. Women who often, against the odds, had made it to the heights of achievement and were being recognised. And now I was being celebrated by them. This was the most amazing experience and professional accolade. I stood there, in my own truth, to thank them and all those who had helped to get me there.

by Jo Cavanagh

Life continues with more opportunities and challenges to meet, celebrations to enjoy and new life coming into the world surrounded by love and a family who will always be there for them. To my inner child, I have been able to offer consolation that the failings of adults were not her fault. To my grown children and grandchildren, I commit my unconditional love. To the children of the world, I wish we would all do better. And to Jackie, I wonder where you are now. With all my heart, I hope you too found your secure and loving place in life.

Nada *Matijevic*

Nada Matijevic believes that our true success starts within ourselves, with knowing who we are and what's important to us, and that our own self-empowerment starts by taking on a leadership role in our lives and careers. But this wasn't always the case.

She realised this after years of moulding herself to fit external forces, which left her yearning for something more from her career.

The journey to a more meaningful career and life has not been straightforward, or without challenges. A desire to realise her purpose and potential has driven Nada to challenge and reinvent herself through a number of career transitions.

Those very challenges that pushed her out of her comfort zones and beyond her perceived boundaries now enable her to help others to be more resourceful and empowered in our rapidly changing world of work.

As a Career Development and Transition Consultant and the founder of Elevate Me, Nada works with professionals and executives who not only want to overcome their career challenges, but to empower and elevate themselves to thrive in career and life.

2015 was a pivotal point in Nada's life, when the desire to be true to herself, her values and purpose led her to make this most significant career change. It meant leaving a well-established and successful career in the professional services and corporate world and going solo, so as not to have to compromise.

Nada is a member of the Career Development Association of Australia and is an MBTI Personality Type and Strong Interest Inventory Certified Practitioner. She holds a Bachelor of Business Studies in Accounting and as a member of CPA Australia is actively involved in supporting members' professional and personal development through the Women's CPA Network Committee.

Outside of work, Nada loves to connect with family, friends and nature, and to spend time with her grandchildren, helping them to discover their own self-identity and potential.

She values individuality and diversity and also loves making a personal connection with people around values and interests that resonate.

Email | nada@elevateme.com.au
LinkedIn | www.linkedin.com/in/nadamatijevic
Website | www.elevateme.com.au
Offer | Take my free online Career Health Diagnostic
https://form.jotform.co/ElevateMe/career-health-diagnostic-1

by Nada Matijevic

Success starts Within

My day had started like many others before it at EY. My work routine was structured and orderly. I was guided by clear performance metrics and utilisation targets which quickened my pace considerably. I was comfortable in my role. It was both demanding and heartening to know what was expected of me and which boxes I needed to tick to succeed.

But soon, an unexpected revelation at a professional development workshop would remove my blinkers forever and lead me to reassess my identity and my work.

The workshop's facilitator conducted a personality profiling exercise. As a consequence, we were all grouped according to our innate similarities and differences. Well... most of us were grouped. I was all alone in one corner of the room. My colleagues largely concentrated in another.

This had me confused and in denial. We were opposites. At a deeper level it meant that my chosen career and I were misaligned. No, that can't be right!

"The big 4 consulting firms commonly hire for one type of profile," the facilitator explained. (This was the 90's, before EY had become the diversity and inclusion champion it is today.) Regardless, the exercise proved to me I had moulded myself externally to fit that profile. Yet deep down, I was me.

My rare part-time role arose because my out-of-the-box thinking manager wanted to try something different. With that move, he and EY won my loyalty. As a returning-to-work-mum, it was an opportunity to reclaim my confidence and my career after the early family-raising years. It meant changing career paths from financial accounting to tax, learning new skills, identifying new opportunities and regaining the professional ground lost while raising my children. But making myself fit in due to the loyalty I felt meant the accumulation of time denying who I was.

Was it a good move? A bad move? These answers are never simple. Yet standing alone in my corner of the workshop accompanied only by a sudden deeper awareness of self was forcing me to ask even harder questions.

- What would I do with this newfound awareness?
- Would it make me leave my safe cocoon and venture into the unknown?
- Would it delay or stop altogether my chances of advancement?
- How were the people in the other corner now regarding me?

The Reflection

That discussion with the psychologist sparked a desire to fully understand myself and my purpose. It set me on a life-long quest of self-discovery, self-empowerment and self-actualisation.

And it meant first going back to my roots...

As a child growing up in a small European country town, I was free, curious and creative. I found joy in interacting with the natural world. I observed everything was connected, had purpose and picked up some important beliefs and values.

My father showed me how, with a flexible mindset and some resourcefulness, any problem could be solved. He, along with my mother, instilled in me a "study hard, work hard" ethic.

My interests led me to the Applied Economics and Organisational Behaviour career path. Unfortunately, recession and poor economic outlook was a curve ball I had not anticipated and made me switch to the safer pathway of Business Studies and Accounting. Looking back now, I can see how I had felt the need to adapt to changing circumstances rather than be me.

From my new vantage point in the corner of the room, I could suddenly see where those gut instincts of flexibility and adaptation had come from. But were they helpful or harmful? For many strengths, if overplayed, have a shadow side.

In the reporting-of-past-and-present-numbers world of accounting, I craved a people connection. My environment valued conformity and uniformity. I valued new ideas and individuality. Though I saw future possibilities and potential improvements, I felt misunderstood or my ideas went unheard.

Despite knowing this career path wasn't my ideal fit, I wasn't ready to make a radical change. I lacked clarity and direction as I had more questions than answers. Instead, I stayed and became more determined to make it work.

by Nada Matijevic

Successes and Setbacks

My interest in human development grew, and wherever I could, I chose this pathway for my professional development. Doing this enabled me to make better-aligned role choices within EY.

I found more fulfilment in management accounting. It enabled me to be more interpretative, change focused and improvements driven. It provided more people contact and opportunity to develop relationships and stakeholder management skills at all levels. I got involved in staff development, team building initiatives and performance management systems.

That kept me engaged, enabled me to build new skills and achieve manager level. However, as I approached my 12th year at EY, and despite the successes, something was still missing. I knew there was more to me that didn't get a chance to be expressed, but it was hard to make the decision to leave a great employer.

Then, life's circumstances forced my next career move, in the form of restructure and role redundancy. Even though I knew I had outgrown both my role and EY, it was still a blow to my confidence and loyalty. Going through redundancy was a career low point… and an opportunity.

Once I regained my perspective, it was quite liberating. A blessing in disguise. The decision had been made. I no longer had to agonise over it. The golden handcuffs were off, I was free to see new possibilities. The support and resources to guide my next move were a bonus. The prospect of charting a new path of my own choosing became exciting.

And just as I found the courage to leave the safety of the cocoon, my resolution was tested by an offer to stay and take another role. But the door had been opened and the view to the outside was tantalising. I had already made a mental leap over the threshold and wanted the new opportunities.

Stretching my Wings

The challenge of trying something new in a different industry and environment appealed to me. Genuine rapport with the hiring manager sealed the deal.

To say my first week at my new large ASX listed employer was a bit of a culture shock would be an understatement. Transitioning here from a professional services environment was like stepping into another world. It required me to adapt and change my approach.

New challenges tested my limits. In particular, using disjointed legacy systems to run a complex procurement rebate process that impacted the whole organisation in a very visible way was intense. Doing it without a proper handover was terrifying. Accomplishing it without (seemingly) missing a beat was rewarding. (At least that's how it appeared on the surface. Below water... I was paddling like crazy!)

I would have been quite happy to settle into a comfort phase in this role. But then my manager dropped a bombshell one day. He said he'd be leaving and had already recommended me for his commercial management procurement role.

My self-doubts immediately surfaced. "I'm not ready, there's so much more to learn," I said. He convinced me to step up to the challenge. The support and mentorship of my new manager empowered me further. So I stretched my wings and flew.

It came down to a simple mindset shift. I went from "I can't" to "let's see what I'm capable of." After that, my determination and hard work ethic pushed me through the barriers.

This allowed me to feel a sense of accomplishment in being able to develop people and collaborative teams. It was fabulous when this was noticed by others in the organisation.

But my team and I weren't the only ones changing. The organisation had changed too through leadership restructures, conflict and aggressive targets to fend off take-over threats. To me though, much of it looked like battling egos and political manoeuvring.

As an indirect consequence of the turmoil, a dark cloud hung over me one beautiful spring day. I saw for the first time within myself the shadow side of a strong work ethic. People were burning out all around me and so was I. I became snappy and irritable with my staff and regretted it deeply. I felt suffocated in the grip of my inner turmoil, caught between having to toe the company line and wanting to do what was right by people. I felt powerless to change things and imprisoned by circumstances beyond my control.

That inner turmoil was my cue… it was time to walk. My strengths of perseverance and hard work were now working against me and those around me. This was upsetting my deeper values.

Catalyst for Change

I was determined to keep evolving by developing a broader skillset and to make more of an impact through leadership. A general management role at a mid-sized property services company surfaced. It appealed as it offered lots of variety and would require me to utilise my diverse mix of skills and experience. However, it was my organisational and people skills that would be called on the most and this challenge attracted me.

It was a turbulent and risky stage of the company's evolution. A year of internal conflict had climaxed in an ownership break-up leaving staff loyalties divided and engagement and morale damaged. This was damaging the brand and client confidence. Additionally, a lot of goodwill and critical know how would be departing as the founders were exiting the business. It dawned on me one day early on in my time there... my position was created to stop the company unravelling. I was the glue.

I remember thinking, maybe sticking with my original study choice of Organisational Behaviour would have been sensible!

I remember experiencing a series of competing thoughts and questions. Could I pull this off? What happens if I fail? The stakes are high. Good people are relying on me to get this right so there's no time to indulge in self-doubt. And finally... Dig deep, Nada, you've got this.

In this highly regulated and competitive industry, I needed to get up to speed quickly. I was responsible for the company's Integrated Management System and importantly, the OH&S, Quality and Environmental accreditations would soon be due for audit and recertification.

So I did what needed to be done even when it pushed me well out of my comfort zone... like attending on-site toolbox meetings and walk-throughs on high-rise rooftops. And me – with a fear of heights!

The work wasn't easy but rising to the challenges was personally rewarding. It expanded my capabilities and confidence. I left a stable, profitable and growing company after two years with a sense of accomplishment. Staff were engaged, management were focussed and clients were regaining confidence in the brand.

Before starting in this role, it hadn't occurred to me being a woman in a senior role in the construction and property services industry would be unconventional. Conventional in this setting, I would learn, was an ingrained culture and vastly different management styles than I was accustomed to. The impact on the people side of the equation required damage control and caused constant HR headaches. Though the underlying people problems were fixable through training and personal development, I hadn't anticipated the strength of the boys' club loyalty and their resistance to change.

This experience reinforced my belief that technical skills and the ability to generate revenue are not enough on their own. People skills and emotional intelligence are important at all levels, particularly in leadership roles.

So with reinvigorated clarity and conviction, I took a giant leap of faith...

Reconnecting with My Purpose

Many people think of starting their own businesses and there are so many factors that need to be taken into account before one does. At that point in my life, one of these factors was like a sunrise guiding me to the light...

Without superior people skills and emotional intelligence levels, too many people would fail to achieve their best capabilities, whether they're employees, leaders or business owners.

And with that, Elevate Me was born. It's my career consulting business where the focus is on elevating others. Working with people who want to evolve and realise their potential is extremely important to me. As is not being hindered from putting people first by conflicting organisational goals.

The decision to leave a well-established career and a well-paid senior role for self-employment wasn't easy and came with obvious risks. Would I regret it later? What if it didn't work out? These questions played out in my mind and had to be dealt with.

Venturing into the unknown world of entrepreneurship would require many new skills. Going from having a team of people sharing the load to having to learn completely new things like setting up a website and system automation was hard.

Reconnecting with why I was doing this sustained me many times. My why was a strong belief in empowering people's potential so they could take a leadership role to drive positive change in their lives and through their careers.

The journey has not been linear or conventional. But all the challenges, twists and turns provided just the insights and skills needed for this, my most meaningful role. Here I can blend my adaptability, creativity, big-picture, possibilities-driven ideas and right-brain people ideals with logical and organised left-brain practicalities to guide decision-making, planning and implementation.

It has enabled me to relate to different workplace challenges, see possibilities amidst uncertainty and chaos and have the structure and discipline to provide an effective framework and implementable system.

Having goals that are aligned with our purpose and values is intrinsically fulfilling and meaningful. Finding our inner drivers and the potential that lies beyond our comfort zones allows us to evolve and self-actualise.

For me, deep and meaningful connection, human evolution and driving positive change is fulfilling and intrinsically rewarding. But we're all unique and need to find our own drivers.

It's a privilege to be part of someone's journey. Moving them from feeling stuck and unhappy to having a compelling purpose-driven vision and the clarity, resources and focus to make it a reality brings unfathomable rewards to me.

I'm still adapting and evolving as the world throws up new challenges. By constantly adapting our perspectives and resourcefulness, we can all turn challenges into opportunities. Thanks, Dad… that one has stayed with me.

It's not always easy. But being able to bring all of me to my work and to live authentically and in alignment with who I am, makes it all the more worthwhile. To me, making a meaningful difference, one person at a time, is priceless.

Self-Evolution

I feel like I've turned full circle since that conversation with the psychologist so many years ago when I was out of touch with myself and not confident in my capabilities.

Since then, I've gone from not wanting to stand out for my differences, lest they be considered weaknesses, to fully embracing them. This has naturally evolved into doing my life's work and to helping others to do theirs.

Life's circumstances throw us curve balls, especially today, in our rapidly changing world. A flexible mindset helps us stay adaptable and resilient, see challenges as opportunities, stretch and grow our capabilities and confidence.

It's through our self-evolution that we elevate and empower ourselves and help shape the future we want. Relying only on our past technical training and experience puts us at risk of getting left behind.

My role and environment no longer define me, I shape them around me. I no longer give away my power to others to make career decisions for me. I take control of deciding my own path and working towards it. Before I could help others, I needed to evolve and empower myself first.

My career drivers definitely have not been conventional or been about maintaining the status quo. Depending on one's vantage point, perhaps my journey was left of field or perhaps it was my destination. What I do know is that everything changed when I discovered my True North and used my inner compass to guide me there.

Now I get to help people connect with who they are, what they want to do and to see possibilities and the steppingstones to achieving that. Their pathway may or may not be direct and linear. It might be a series of steppingstones or one huge leap. The important thing is to see possibilities and options and to make decisions with conviction.

It starts with getting to know yourself and being true to that person. If you're grounded in who you are, what you stand for and the impact you want to make, you'll know which direction to choose, when to stay and when to walk away.

by Nada Matijevic

The important thing is to take on a leadership role in your life and career and not leave it to destiny. The world needs good leaders right now and now is always the best time to step up to the plate.

Di
Coad

You know, Di never did follow the rules! Establishing her own path in both life and business with many highs and lows to go along with it, but Property Management is in her blood!

Di is extremely fortunate to have some amazing ladies to work with her, that come along for the ride of new business ideas every other week. Di has recently taken on the challenge of diversifying the business into Airbnb Management, with more to come...

As well as experiences mentioned in this book, Di has also raised over $8,000 for the Royal Children's Hospital burns unit by trekking both The Great Wall of China and the Himalayas, which stemmed from spending time in the burn's unit as a child.

From a personal point of view, Di and her husband recently relocated from Melbourne to the Macedon Ranges in Victoria and are in the midst of planning to build their dream home, they also own two investment properties which helps her in providing advice to her clients from an owner perspective. Di genuinely loves to help people with every part of their investment journey and help guide other business owners starting out.

In her rare moments away from work, Di enjoys going to Flemington & Moonee Valley races, loves her coffee and a red wine or three, boxing, pilates and going hiking with her husband and very active Border Collie Maisy.

Next on the trek list... The Inca Trail... one day!

Facebook business | facebook.com/coadrealestate
Facebook personal | facebook.com/coadmacedon

Never did follow the Rules

So there I was... staring bankruptcy in the face after just a month in business.

I like to think I was always meant to be a business owner because, as a kid, I was always dreaming big. Though, at the time, my dreams were more around being a princess than the business owner. And back then, well, I seemed to have lots of time to dream...

The fragility of my two older brothers' health and their natural abilities coupled with a lack of any amazing personal talents on my part, forced me into the strange situation of having to grow up a little tougher than I might have otherwise. You see, my parents were always driving my brothers around to various sporting or musical engagements where they shone or to the skin specialist. Whereas there never seemed to be enough of a need for me to be taken anywhere as there was insufficient talent or illness to warrant the journey. So I just tagged along and sat on the sidelines. You see, I wasn't smart at school, gifted at music and nor did I excel at sport.

Well... at least I was a good sport! With plenty of opportunities to dream...

by Di Coad

Dad worked all the time (at one point I remember counting four jobs!) and Mum was a housewife. Every weekend, we all followed my brothers around to various sporting or musical events which left no time or money for anything I might be interested in.

However, Dad did instil in me a gift for which I will be forever grateful; the desire to work hard.

He got my brothers their first jobs and offered me the same opportunity. Determined to find my own way, I declined the offer. So imagine how proud of myself I was when I got a job at Dandenong Library! Many found this amusing because I have a loud voice and personality, so me with the silent job of stacking library books on shelves was hard for some to comprehend. However, the library was more than just a job; it was an escape from being bullied as the 'fat girl' at high school. It was a sanctuary where I could go about my tasks.

Above all – I got paid $32 a fortnight! I still have my first pay cheque.

After school & library work, I started an Associate Diploma in TAFE and actually started applying myself with what was then known as Desktop Publishing. Finally, I'd found something that I was good at and a little self-belief started to develop.

While at TAFE, I also wanted to keep earning money so I did administration work for some quite big companies through a temp agency. This opened my eyes to the fast-paced corporate world. I LOVED it!

After TAFE, I kept up with temp work as I didn't really have any idea what I wanted to do with my new qualification. Back then, there weren't job websites, just the Herald Sun for positions vacant.

And one of those ads leapt out at me one day – a real estate receptionist position.

I wasn't particularly looking for real estate work. I'd have taken anything permanent in reception or administration at the time, so it seemed like the right fit.

Looking back, I was quite a big girl then. At 50kgs overweight, my first boss had to look past my shape and recognise my skills. He had to see that I was worthy of a chance and the effort. In short, he had to do what my parents did not. Ian was a fine man who took a risk – he was putting me on the front desk in an industry where appearance is everything.

And WOW! Did my eyes POP!
Real Estate was awesome!!

Real estate in the late 90's was phrenetic. We were listing 20 auctions a weekend! It was insane. I loved being busy and loved being part of the team. My talents were in demand and my self-assurance grew. I spent a year working 13-day fortnights and completely changed my lifestyle. Like the ugly duckling, I was transforming from the fat girl that got bullied into someone who felt valued by people I respected. I lost those 50kgs and found a confidence in my work and myself that I never knew existed.

After 3 years of this, I developed what has become the familiar pattern of a rut. Not happy in Melbourne, I began looking for the next thing. At that time, December 1999, I hadn't travelled anywhere. I had met some people from Perth through friends and decided that it sounded like a fun lifestyle. I left for Perth to live in 2001.

My Mum was very critical of this because the first-time leaving home was to the other side of the country! In 2001, this was almost unheard of when flights were about $900 each way. I have learnt over time I never seemed to take the conventional route. So, even though I worked my way up from receptionist to office manager, it was time to move on. Looking back, this was probably also a bit of a 'stuff you' to my Mum who said I couldn't do it. Proving that I could do it and not being overshadowed by my brothers was important to me.

Perth was fun! I was 23 year old, met a boy and got a job easily in real estate. I ended up moving around within that company until I was a PA for a high-profile agent. We didn't get along and they moved me on.

The Perth real estate market was slower than what I was used to, so it was hard to adapt. I had to find other ways of occupying myself...

Party time!

Without the necessity to work long hours, I experienced an unfamiliar freedom. So now I was big on having all that fun that I hadn't been having in Melbourne. In Perth, I was there for the lifestyle, which wasn't great for my budding career, but was a heck of a lot of fun...

Perth ended up just being three years of my life, because, fun though it was, my life was imploding there. I was partying way too much, fell in with the wrong people after the boyfriend relationship breakdown and I couldn't hold down a job to save myself. To secure employment, I moved from real estate to telecommunications. Even though this was a great job, I was spiralling downward with all the partying and needed to leave Perth. So with a friend from Melbourne, I went backpacking around to top end of Australia, in a Nissan Pulsar.

That sounds fun, right?

It was. Renee and I were mid-twenties, dressed in skimpy skirts and bikinis and went off touring the top end. What could go possibly wrong?

We certainly had some awesome experiences... encounters with emu's and crocodiles and nearly colliding with road-trains to name a few. All in all, it was a wonderful experience until Renee had to go back to work and my money ran out.

I was determined at this point to get back on my own two feet. The fun was done. I had to find a job! I arrived in Brisbane without a clue about where to go or what to do. Thankfully, I had one friend there from Perth and got a job with the same telecommunications company as before. I also had to get a second job to pay back some loans I had accumulated. So real estate reception work re-entered my life. Yep... it was back doing 13-day fortnights.

I stayed in Brisbane for seven years, finding my ambition again for an industry I truly love. I went from weekend receptionist, to BDM, to Property Manager and on to Department Manager in three short years. I worked hard to prove myself and shook off my partying which had become a problem.

In 2007, I was given the opportunity to be with a national brand running their rent roll. I started off managing Brisbane, then Queensland, then NSW, then SA. They also moved me to Adelaide for 6 months. So at that time I went back to study and added to my real estate qualifications. Now I was certified in WA, SA and my full license in Qld, NSW & Vic. I stayed in this role for a little longer and was there for just on 3 years... until I got bullied out by new male senior managers.

I've never been one to differentiate between males and females in the workplace. Yet after 3 years, they had tripled my workload and I had turned around a $40k a month loss to $20k a month profit with no pay rise. I wrote a proposal for why I should get one. It was declined. In tears, I left. That was my first experience of giving a large company everything I could, including uprooting my life and going interstate for them, and receiving nothing back.

At this point, I found that I couldn't settle. It was a chance conversation which led to me becoming a partner in a real estate office! I stayed with Tracie for just over a year and tried to build the rent roll. But I found Brisbane wasn't for me anymore and it was time to move home.

So here I was again... no job, not a lot of money, no house and my fifth interstate move in 10 years. Oh dear.

Head down, bum up again. In my first few years back, I went through a couple of jobs, trusted the wrong people and got burnt along the way. It was a high-pressure time where I was micro-managed by the wrong people from big companies and for three years I loathed going to work.

Skip to 2013. An opportunity to buy a rent roll presented itself. I had no plan and no money but saw this as my ticket out of the doldrums I was in professionally. Enough was enough – I had to change my trajectory!

I thought I knew pressure and stress. Then I bought a business! The first 3-4 years were a nightmare, scrambling to keep the business afloat. I learnt very quickly how to run a business, albeit a sinking business. So I put on my big girl panties and tapped into a place I didn't know I had. There

I found the courage to stick with this business and not let it sink.

I didn't have the funds to buy this business outright so was introduced to a private investor who topped up the balance that I couldn't borrow from a bank. Now with someone else involved, I knew I had to give this everything. Shortly after, the truth of what I was involved in came down on me like a tonne of bricks…

Another agent in the area had a copy of the client list that I had paid a lot of money for and was stealing the clients! This agent was a disaffected employee of the seller.

So there I was… staring bankruptcy in the face after just a month in business. At the time, I was unaware that I should have written a retention clause in the contract. The outcome? Clients from the rent roll I purchased were leaving, I was in debt because of them and there was nothing I could do about it.

After 60 properties had been taken away (approx. $100k/pa income) I literally had to beg the other agency to stop. They agreed as they had proved their point with the seller. But it didn't hurt him. He had his money. It hurt me.

Running alongside this, the seller wouldn't sign over the office lease to me so I then faced eviction from the office. I figured that if he wouldn't sign the lease over and neither would the agent, then why should I pay rent there if the debt is not in my name? It was the first smart move I'd made! So after finding a new office, I ripped out all my improvements from the old one and left.

The next few years were spent scrambling to keep clients while the situation was deteriorating. You see, it was becoming clear the seller had substance abuse issues (we even had to breathalyse him before signing the contracts!) and he went to a competitor, even though it was against the contract terms. Without a care in the world, he started approaching my clients. One of my now favourite clients came in one day to pick up her files and leave after the lies she was told about me by the seller. I remember crying and wondering if it would ever end.

These personal attacks were devastating.

I could either take it lying down or level the playing field. I chose the latter and told the clients that came to me the truth about what had happened so far. Thankfully, they trusted me and gave me a chance. 8 years later, they are still with me and have given me more properties to manage as well as referrals to friends.

During this period of vulnerability, I had listened to the wrong people telling me I couldn't do it on my own. Not trusting myself, I got into a franchise with a big brand that had an office on St Kilda Road. Things looked really good on the outside, but they were imploding on the inside... again.

On top of everything else, the two team members I had left. I knew I couldn't do this on my own, so I asked a friend I knew from Brisbane, to come help me with some temp work. Six years later, she's still with me and we're now a team of 5 and I couldn't do this without Deanne's support and my ever-growing team of strong amazing women!

During this period, I had met my wonderful man, Wayne. He is amazing and has supported me as I spent years keeping angry creditors at bay, trying to keep clients and replace the lost clients. He stayed with me through thick and thin.

By 2015, clients were coming and going. I had issues with previous employers, issues with the seller, the accountant I was using at the time was charging exorbitant amounts that I couldn't keep up with, I fell behind in payments with the investor, I was struggling emotionally and the pressure was enormous. Ultimately, it all boiled down to one thing... I realised I simply had to stop trusting advice of the wrong people. I could trace most of the problems back to when I had taken such advice. It was time to start making my own decisions. I had become sick and tired of the stories I was hearing about myself. People were calling me a 'silly young girl," and a "f-ing idiot who has no idea!" This made me all the more determined to prove them wrong. I always knew real estate agents could be sharks, but this was a whole new level!

This went on for 2 years. I was constantly treading water to keep my head above it. Things became so tight, the bank started visiting my office and threatening to pull the loan for the business.

Then came the devastating news that my Mum was diagnosed with bowel cancer. Life was throwing lemons and I didn't feel like making lemonade. She and I had our issues over the years, but all that had disappeared over time. I didn't share with my parents what was happening with the business, as I'm certain I would've been berated. With the diagnosis though, there suddenly seemed to be more important things to worry about.

Sadly, in 2017, my 67 year old Mum lost her battle. In January, Mum was told she had 6mths, as the cancer had won over her. I wanted her to see me walk down the aisle, so Wayne and I agreed to marry in April. Four days after I told her we were engaged, she departed this world. The wedding went ahead with Dad's blessing. So while scrambling in the business, we put a wedding together for 80 people in 32 days. Out of pride, Dad paid for a funeral and a wedding within a month. I often say now, "If you want something done, ask a busy person." Wayne also settled on an investment property in those 32 days, so I was grieving, getting married and settling on properties… all in a month.

I told you I don't follow the rules, right?

Things are now at some level of normality. Years before it became a thing, I closed my shopfront, left the franchise that I couldn't afford, became my own brand and moved to a home-office. Though the other agents tried to bully me against this last development, I resisted the temptation to listen to their fear-driven advice. The fact was, I knew no one came in for rental or sales lists, just tradies for keys so it wasn't worth the rent and other outgoings. I went against the grain again, and it was the best thing I'd done since buying the business. I have a sign in my office that reads "The greatest pleasure in life, is doing what people say you cannot do." I really believe that.

Now, the business has doubled in size in the last 12mths. We bought out the investor and bought another rent roll in the Macedon Ranges. We are growing steadily now, and all our business is referrals, not marketing. After everything, I really do enjoy helping people and love being a Property Manager and business owner. It provides a variety I love and am one of a small number of sole female business owners in this industry. It's a very hard job with lots of hours, but it's also very rewarding.

I am blessed with an amazing team, clients and the most amazing husband & fur-baby Border Collie, Maisy. I guess there really are silver linings, right?

Work hard, be good to yourself, listen to your own advice and the rewards will follow.

Kim *Downes*

Kim Downes was born and raised on the outskirts of Chicago, a place she never felt like she fit in for various reasons.

As a child, she and her closet cousin would dream and fantasize about a land down under. And in 1993 she moved to this glorious country. Guess that's what happens when you put your dreams in the hands of the Universe.

Between Church, school and University the concept of giving and service to others was a part of everyday life. This was something that came naturally and was something she enjoyed. Upon graduating from University, she took a job at a Not for Profit and has never looked at another industry. Her passion for helping others and philanthropy was imbedded...

and it was something that never occurred to her that she could do as a "job".

She has been a philanthropy and fundraising strategist for over 30 years assisting Not for Profits develop a culture of philanthropy and become sustainable. Her specific speciality is in working with female donors and teaching organisations the role and influence of women in Australian philanthropy. Since the age of 18 she has also made sure that volunteering is a part of her life.

Website	www.kimberlydownes.com
Facebook	Kim Weber Downes
Instagram	kimmiedmelb
LinkedIn	linkedin.com/in/kimberly-downes-cfre-cap-emfia-45664534

by Kim Downes

Trust your Instincts

It was 9pm on Tuesday, 30 July 2012. A night that would change me forever.

I was watching television with my 13 and 15-year-old children when the doorbell rang. I blurted out, "Oh shit! That's the doctor and it isn't going to be good news." It was my fear talking and I immediately wanted to suck those words back in when I realised the kids were looking at me with panic growing in their eyes.

For eight months leading up to that fateful Tuesday night, I had been seeing the GP every Monday morning with migraines that were now 24/7. I had tried every drug you can think of to get rid of them, but nothing was working. At the end of July, I was driving back from a client in Ballarat when my eyesight went. I could still see, but everything was in triplicate. I had to close one eye at a time to drive. Not the wisest thing. Yet pushing through and not creating a fuss was what I always did.

It's how I'd been programmed.

I answered the door with children at my side. My husband was in New Zealand for work at the time so

by Kim Downes

I knew I had to be strong for the kids. I was right... it was my doctor. He gave me the classic line, "I have good news and I have bad news. The good news is we know what IT is. The bad news is you are seeing a neurosurgeon tomorrow."

IT... was a brain tumour.

When he said those words, the strangest thing happened to me. A wave of relief washed over me. Yes, relief. Funny thing to feel when you've just been told you have a brain tumour, right?

But you see, it was a thing. Something you could look at and point to. It was real. So there was no reason for self-doubt any more. And no longer did I need to endure others who doubted me.

For the next 20 minutes, the doctor looked at the CT scans and talked about the appointment with the neurosurgeon. I confess, that part was a blur because FINALLY people would believe my pain was real. I wasn't making it up. I was only sorry my kids were standing right there listening to every word.

I called my husband to give him the news. He panicked and couldn't get home fast enough. He got on the first flight he could the next day.

A brain tumour.

I slept like a baby that night.

I had an answer and was so grateful.

You see, after months of headaches and constant pain I had an answer. After months of being told "just relax" or "stress is causing your headaches" I had an answer. After months of self-doubt, I had an answer! It was liberating. I was out of the prison I and others had created.

There was no questioning that I would push through this and there was no time for a pity party. There wasn't even time to think of what I was about to go through. I had things to organise for everyone else! Why did I sleep like a baby that night? Because for years I was doubting if I was to blame for my symptoms. After all, no one believed me and everyone was saying I was bringing the headaches on myself. At one stage we were on holidays in Fiji with friends and halfway through the trip I could barely walk because I was so dizzy with pain. Everyone's reaction was, what on earth are you stressing about when we are on this beautiful holiday?

Now I had an answer. It wasn't my fault.

Was I doing too much? Maybe. I was a mum, a wife, I worked fulltime as a consultant, I was a volunteer on a few committees and I tried to make time to look after myself after all the chores were done and everyone else was looked after.

Isn't that what Mum's do?

A strange thing occurred to me, from a young age I always had this feeling I would die young. Was this my time? And define young? Or was it just a fear of dying? I couldn't answer any of that, but it was certainly in the back of my mind.

I grew up in a family on the outskirts of Chicago where a strong work ethic was instilled in us kids and there was no time for slacking. Just imagine the combination of an Italian father and an Irish mother... chores were the priority and perfection was the standard. Perhaps if everything was done perfectly there would be no arguing when Dad got home from work. So I grew up pushing through everything and not making a fuss. I learnt to blend into the background and never stand out. I valued doing things for others and not for myself.

The doctors believed the tumour has been growing for at least ten years. I had just thought it was the migraines getting worse and more frequent. Or that it was hormones. Funny how a conditioned response can imperil you.

Just push through, don't cause a fuss...

When I met with the neurosurgeon on Wednesday, he was busy explaining the tumour's location and how it was wrapping itself around main arteries. Due to this, it was imperative the surgery happen right away. But, as he was describing the procedure, I was busy flipping through my diary. He stopped me and said, "What are you doing?"

I responded, "Well, I am trying to figure out when I can fit the surgery in... I think December might work."

He rolled his eyes. "You will be admitted to the hospital tomorrow and surgery will be on Friday or you will have a major stroke this weekend."

But see... there was a problem. I was chairing a major fundraising ball for my daughters' school that weekend. Though, truthfully all I could think was, "What a relief, now I don't have to worry about what to wear." I contacted the committee right away and then got on with organising the kid's schedules, the laundry and ironing and my client work. I thought for sure by Monday I'd be back on schedule and everyone would hardly notice my absence.

The whole situation seemed surreal. I didn't even get on Google to research the tumour or what to expect after surgery. I didn't look up my neurosurgeon to find out his qualifications. I was coping by pretending it wasn't happening. I'd go in, they'd take it out and, poof! I'd be fine and back to normal – headache free.

But hang on... brain tumours happen to other people, not me.

It wasn't until I was in my room at the hospital that I realised there was no turning back. This was actually happening to me and the diagnosis was just an answer to a question. Now... something had to be done about it!

It's true what they say...you will never have a situation you are not strong enough to handle but how we handle it teaches us a lot about who we are and our character. On the outside I looked strong to everyone but on the inside, I was a little girl wanting to curl up in my Daddy's lap and hide from the world.

Before the surgery, the head of the neurosurgery department, whom I knew, came in to see me. He looked around the room and saw the stack of books on the table and asked, "What is that?"

I declared I had work to do.

He gave me an evil eye then looked at my husband and said, "Take that home please. She won't be doing any work for a while."

That's when the revelation hit me. For some reason, I was determined to show everyone this was just a speedbump. This was not going to slow me down or define me. But with hindsight, what was I trying to prove? And to whom? And for what? I don't remember ever receiving a Super Woman cape!

The kids left school early that day and came into the hospital to see me before surgery. Looking at the fear in their eyes is when it hit me. I had to survive this. Dying young wasn't an option. They were still too little to be without a Mum. There was still too much I had to experience with them.

"Please God!" I begged this wasn't actually happening to me. How could this happen to me? So I focused on them and talked about their plans for the weekend and school the next week. I had to protect my babies.

"It's time," said the nurse. "The surgeon is ready for you." I hugged my kids and husband so tightly, praying it wouldn't be for the last time. Brain surgery was serious. This was really happening. And it was happening to me.

Outside the operating theatre, the orderly was chatting to me and making jokes. I truly appreciated his efforts. As time stood still though, I tried not to think about what was beyond those doors. All I wanted to do was get up and run away.

Once in the operating theatre, my neurosurgeon was very serious and going through his last-minute checks. I shouted to him, "Hey Ian, you can't start yet. The whole team isn't here."

He stopped what he was doing, looked around the operating theatre and did a head count.

"Who's missing?"

"My stylist."

He laughed. "Sorry darling, I am afraid I am your stylist and I'll admit I'm a much better neurosurgeon than I am a stylist".

I had to laugh because the alternative was to cry. After all, laughter and making jokes was my defence mechanism, the only way I'd learned to cope with stressful situations. And this one topped the charts for stress levels.

As the surgery team was getting ready to put me under, I grabbed the hand of the anaesthetist and my neurosurgeon and squeezed. Looking them both in the eyes, I said, "Please… I must wake up to see my children." That was the last thing I remember.

"What time is it?" I shouted as I came to.

The nurses gently made me lay back down and explained that surgery took two hours longer than expected and my surgeon was talking with my husband.

I was awake! I was alive! That's all I could think. I was so grateful.

It was a rough night though. I was in a lot of pain and the nurses were in constantly checking on me. But if I could get through the surgery, I could get through anything.

By 6am the next morning, I was calling home. I was telling my husband where to find my son's footy gear for the game that day and reminding him of the schedule for the weekend. My son's school had told him he didn't have to play the mandatory Saturday sport that day, but I'm told he played the best game of his life for his Mum. My little hero.

When my husband came to see me on Saturday afternoon, he didn't bring the kids. He wanted to take a picture of me first then show the kids so they were prepared for what I looked like. To be honest, I wasn't even sure I was prepared for what I looked like…

Swollen eye, half a shaved head and a bit black and blue.

My neurosurgeon was correct, he was a better neurosurgeon than stylist.

On Sunday when my family visited, my little boy

stood in the furthest corner of the room with sadness in his eyes. My girl seemed brave. They were afraid to hug me because they didn't want to hurt me. All I wanted to do was squeeze them tight.

What I didn't quite grasp at that time was that phase one, the operation, was over. We were now all holding our breath for phase two.... the pathology results. It took a few more days for those to arrive. When they came, the news was wonderful. As my neurosurgeon took his time and removed the entire tumour, I wouldn't need any more treatment for a stage two tumour. I was so, so grateful.

Everything happens for a reason. And if no other reason can be found, then my fallback reason is that everything can teach me something. And this one certainly did in terms of the reactions of others…

Some people reacted with fear, like I was too fragile to talk to or that I'd break if they got too close. Maybe I was contagious. Maybe they thought I'd changed. One friend even told me she would have come to my funeral.

Unfortunately, I lost friendships over it as people stayed away or wanted me to comfort them because of the fear and anxiety they experienced upon learning of my condition. But how could I comfort others when I was busy trying to work out how to cope myself?

I just wanted to be treated normally.

Conversely, I was overwhelmed with the outpouring of love and support from others who made sure my fridge and freezer were full, the kids had everything they needed and my dog was walked daily. This outpouring of support was something I never expected and wondered why I deserved it. For this support I will be forever grateful as it had a huge impact on me and my family. The human spirit of generosity and kindness lives in most people. It's only the few that spoil it.

About four months after the surgery, my neurosurgeon called me. I froze when I saw his name come up on my phone. Was something else wrong?

"Hi, I need to pick your brain," he said.

"You already did that", I replied. There's me coping with fear again by making jokes!

He wanted to have lunch with me to see if I would be interested in joining the Australian Pituitary Foundation Board, which he chaired. As he put it, I may now have significant value on the board since my skull had been opened. "You see," he explained, "they need an airhead."

Flattery! What's a girl to do?

I was honoured and have been on the board ever since.

I'm still learning to listen to my body and to be gentle with myself as there are some repercussions from the tumour. The best thing is, I don't doubt myself anymore. I know the difference between feeling stressed and when things just aren't right.

Upon reflection I don't think I would have handled the surgery any differently. I did what I knew how to do – push through, be strong for others and not make a fuss so they didn't worry. Looking back now though, I would have been gentler with myself during recovery. I would have put that imaginary Super Woman cape away and tried to stop proving anything to anyone, especially myself. I think, as a woman, I put a little extra pressure on myself as I felt I would be judged, especially in a work situation.

by Kim Downes

I still believe everything happens for a reason. Every time I say this, my family rolls their eyes. But it's true. Everything has something to teach us. Even if it takes us a while to figure out what the lesson is. I've stopped worrying about dying young and instead embrace each day while listening to my body... with a lot more confidence now!

Annie *Milne*

Annie commenced her career in Recruitment in 1994 and over the past 20 years prior to co-founding Sprout Recruitment, Annie held Senior Management roles within some of the worlds largest recruitment organisations including Select, Manpower and People Infrastructure.

Annie has delivered successful business outcomes for organisations from small family businesses to global organisations across a diverse range of industries.

Holding formal qualifications in Communications, Psychology and Business Management, Annie is passionate about leadership, people and believes that communication is the key to both personal and business success.

When not working, Annie enjoys time with her family and friends on the beautiful NSW Central Coast and has a keen interest in Horse Racing. Annie is passionate about PT by the waterfront and skiing in Winter to maintain balance in a hectic crazy world.

Facebook	www.facebook.com/annie.milne.9
LinkedIn	www.linkedin.com/in/annie-milne-5194916

by Annie Milne

You should buy yourself a Lottery Ticket

The words that will forever stay with me are... "You should buy yourself a lottery ticket."

For as long as I can remember I wanted a life that was different... something a little less ordinary than the humdrum. I started young on this train of thought by wanting to marry David Cassidy or Donny Osmond. Just one of them, I've never been greedy. However, the probability of that occurring was small, especially given my start in life...

I'm the youngest of 3 children by over 15 years. So according to my siblings, I'm the princess and the baby. We grew up in a small cotton and coal mining town in the North of England. Leigh, in Lancashire, is the home of the mighty Cherry and White Centurions and the local delicacy is a dish called lobbie – it really is quite delicious! It's a small town in geography and mindset; a town where the majority are born, work, grow up, marry someone from the same town and live there until they stop breathing. One of the most exciting things in Leigh is the number 26 bus. In 50 minutes, it can have you at the Manchester Arndale Centre where you can shop till you drop.

by Annie Milne

My siblings and I well and truly bucked this small-town trend.

My sister rebelled by daring to move across the Pennines to Yorkshire, where she eventually married the enemy – a Yorkshire man. Heaven forbid! And my brother... well he went completely rogue by working on cruise ships travelling the world! Nothing short of preposterous! How could a life exploring exotic ports be attractive to a boy from Leigh? Eventually he came to his senses though. He returned to Leigh and married a lovely Leigh girl.

As kids, we lived in a modest two-up, two-down terrace house in a nice street. Certainly nothing fancy but nice and respectable. Mum baked on Sundays whilst Dad took me swimming at the local baths. He would then troop myself and my friends to the local park and through the woods. Bluebells are still my favourite flower because of these adventures and remind me of him always.

All good things must come to an end though. My parents separated when I was 7. Mum did the best she could on limited funds. She was, and still is, our rock – hardworking, honest and staunchly protective of our family unit. Throughout school, I was the class-clown but had the smarts to lift my game in fifth form where I got my first leadership role... head prefect. It was my first glimpse of being overworked and underpaid, a pattern I have since mastered. I was amazingly lucky to be provided the opportunity to go on and study Psychology and Performing Arts, the first in our family to study beyond high school. Upon reflection, I can see the huge sacrifices mum made so I could follow that path. At the time, I didn't appreciate it. If I'm really honest, I could have worked harder and played less.

by Annie Milne

Travel was and still is my passion. Bitten by the wanderlust bug early in life, I literally turned my world upside down at 23 to follow my heart. I moved my entire life to the beautiful Central Coast of NSW, leaving behind my amazing family and lifelong friendship group. Initially intending to stay for 3 to 6 months, 30 years later I find myself back here. Really, why would you want to be anywhere else?

They say history repeats and this I believe. Patterns, history (whatever you want to call it) will repeat until you work out what causes you to behave the way you do and make the decisions you make. That said, fast forward 3 years from moving to Australia and my fairy tale was over. I found myself a single parent on the other side of the world, away from my family, friends and support network. Don't get me wrong... this isn't a pity party! The decision to become a single parent was mine and mine alone, much to the disappointment of both families. He and I just weren't meant to be. We were so very young and the responsibility of mortgages and babies crushed the fun out of our relationship. We both deserved so much more than we were giving each other. I left our family home with a mattress, lounge, 2 pans and Kane's cot on a bright October day in 1993. I was full of optimism and hope for adventures new.

Family units come in many shapes and forms. Our new unit came in the shape of Kane and I, my mum, we'll call her granny as everyone does, and my bestie to this day, Poss. When I say we had very little, that was an understatement. So much so that we were busted one night walking home from the pub with armfuls of glasses that we may have acquired from our trusty friends the glass collectors. We were clanking so much that a lovely man who was walking his dog kindly informed us that we were going the wrong way.

by Annie Milne

According to him, the pub was in the other direction. Oh?

For a small moment in time, all was calm. I was working with my bestie locally for a questionable husband and wife team. But a job is a job, right? The cash was average but I had use of a car which, I may or may not have spilled Thai food on the front seat of, and the hours were convenient. We were happy in our new home and life was good. Then, as the story goes… 'twas the night before Christmas and the holidays were one sleep away. I remember vividly walking upstairs to say Merry Christmas to the charming owners of the business and walking down those same stairs unemployed, redundant.

Merry Christmas indeed.

Hindsight is a wonderful thing. At the time, it was the end of the world. I was completely lost. The rug had been well and truly been pulled from under my feet. In reality though, it was the start of my wonderful career in recruitment and a sliding doors event. Now, I'm so amazingly grateful to that pair of awful humans. They really did change my life and teach me valuable lessons on timing and how to be a decent person.

We moved to the big smoke in 1994 because the commute to and from the coast was killing my life. Leaving at 5am and getting home at 7.30pm was just too much. So bags were packed and down the M1 we trooped. The bright lights of Cherrybrook were calling. By 28, I was working hard and moving through the recruitment ranks. I was loving my work as the divisional manager for a recruitment company in Western Sydney, it wasn't unusual for me to be doing 10-12 hours a day. Front and centre of my mind always was knowing that I was working hard to provide a great future for my son and mum who had since relocated from the UK.

by Annie Milne

I had also started to establish new networks and was beginning to find some balance by enjoying some fun times with my friends when Kane was with his dad every other weekend. Responsible servicing of alcohol wasn't on anyone's radar back then and I'm pretty sure our binge drinking on the weekends wasn't a healthy habit. Yet always my drive and focus were to create a sustainable career that would ultimately provide a stable future and lovely life for my family. I wanted to make memories that we would look back on forever – zoo trips, theme parks, fun and laughter all the way. I desperately wanted to give Kane everything I hadn't had.

Work hard play hard, that was the motto of the day.

The first sign that something was wrong was the headaches. Aching, nagging headaches. Then came sensitivity to light, sound and just about everything else. The pain was unbearable. Worst of all... sensitivity to wine! Heaven forbid! One sip brought on the worst pain and tunnel vision and a headache that would send me to bed from arrival time after work to heading back the next day. Yup... you read that right. I carried on working throughout this entire nightmare. Knowing I was working hard, I self-diagnosed without the assistance of Dr Google, given that wasn't even a thing, that I was stressed and tired. So I tried floatation tanks, meditation, CDS, tai chi, candles, herbal tea. You name it, I tried it. "Take a day off work," I hear you yell. Unfortunately, that wasn't in my plan at that point. Instead of getting better, the symptoms were escalating. I started to get the strangest of sensations in my left arm and hand. It felt like my arm was not my own. It felt like a lobster claw and I had constant pins and needles in my hand and fingers. To add insult to injury, I was losing my balance and falling off my heels on the left side. At

by Annie Milne

this point, I finally went to see the doctor. Was that a cheer I heard from you, dear reader? Or a slap around the head!

Over the weeks that followed, they thought I had trapped nerve migraines, allergies and stress. I was prescribed Valium. Wow! I was off my face! That stuff is not for me! When it didn't resolve quickly, the doctor was stumped and sent me to Neurologist Dr Brian Somerville at Westmead for a CT Scan and MRI. Technology wasn't as speedy in the 90's and it took 14 days for the results to come back from my tests. It was the longest of fortnights. The words he said next are forever etched in my memory. "You've had a TIA, a mini-stroke. Consider it a warning and consider yourself very lucky. You should buy yourself a lottery ticket. I thought you had a brain tumour." On that day, I found a new mantra… Live every day as if it were your last. To this day, I have the plaque that I bought that eventful day saying those words.

I would love to say that I woke up one morning and felt better. But no, it was a slow process. I had lost about 12% function on my left side and still fell off my shoes for a good 3 years after. The sensitivity to food and certain drinks subsided as did the migraines and my reliance on Mersyndol.

Over the next 20 years, I went on to have the most amazing career and gave our lovely family the life that I dreamt for us all creating the memories that had always been my ultimate goal. Was it easy? Hell no. Were there amazing highs and lows, heartbreaks, disappointments and celebrations? Indeed. There were enough to fill 10 chapters of a book… in fact many books!

I have learned many lessons. We all do. Now I consider myself to be a bit of a wise owl… still learning, but older and wiser with more vision and hindsight is a wonderful gift. Most who know me would consider me to be fairly high energy with a wicked sense of humour and a smart one-liner ready for most situations. A wonderful leader and mentor I had many years ago once called me on my bullshit. He said, "Do you realise that you use humour to cover your emotions and to distract people away from the real you?" Until that light bulb moment, I really hadn't realised I did. But OMG… I really did in most situations deflect deflect deflect. I can see now that I still do it to some extent, but I'm definitely more mindful these days not to bury a situation and avoid it. My journey has taught me that emotional wounds are just like physical wounds – if you bury them and don't tend to them, they become rancid and fester and poison your mind, body and spirit . You need to address the wounds from your burden basket and tend to them. Then and only then do you begin to heal and learn from the mistakes of your past.

Spirituality has always been something that has been really important to me. It has played a huge part in my personal development since I can remember. Over the past few years, gratitude manifestation and living a good life with abundance have become important elements of the fabric of me. Finding beauty in the everyday was something I once had to really remind myself to do. Now it's just me, a part of who I am. Even on the hardest of days, some are trickier than others, there is beauty to be found all around in nature, in the kindness of others, in the everyday. I challenge you to find something beautiful in the first hour of your day. Sometimes it's the smell of freshly cut grass, freshly brewed coffee, the contrast of the colour of the trees against the sky. Look for these moments and be grateful for the small things.

by Annie Milne

Time for some introspection…

I have made some terrible decisions in my earlier years both personally and professionally that I still look back on and cringe at. I ask myself, "Why did you do that?" Or, "Where was your moral compass when you made that decision?" You can't go back and you can't change what happened in the past. What's done is done. There is nothing to be gained by dwelling and replaying situations and events in your mind yet you can learn from them. I've learned love, friendship and family will sustain you and show you the way home when you are lost and there is nothing else. Embrace and nurture your tribe.

I've learned to take opportunities as they come.

If opportunities come along and excite and challenge you, self-doubt will always be there trying to freak you out. Am I good enough? Can I do this? For what it's worth, take the opportunity and work the details out later. Work hard and learn your craft. Be the go-to. Be the knowledge. Share your knowledge with others wanting to learn, mentor and lead with honesty and humility. Take care of yourself. Listen to yourself and the internal dialogue. If you are tired, rest; hungry, nourish your body. Follow your intuition – if something feels wrong, it probably is. If something seems too good to be true, it probably is. Buy the blueberries, burn the candle, read the book, have the massage, drink the great coffee and wine and wear your best undies. Every day is special and deserves to be celebrated.

Live everyday as if it were your last.

Emma *Hobson*

Regarded as one of Australia's most influential people in the health and beauty industry today, Emma Hobson has spent the last 30 years shaping what she considers to be an industry of women for women.

Her expertise in the areas of dynamic business strategies, leadership & team management along with her unparalleled insight into the future trends of the skin care, wellness and spa industry; have led Emma to appear on stages all over the world and be featured regularly in many high profile publications.

In her current role as Education Director for The International Dermal Institute and Dermalogica (APAC), Emma has had the opportunity to help thousands of small to medium sized business owners succeed in the multibillion-dollar aesthetic sector.

Her passion for helping women in business is equal to her love for the industry she has personally grown up in from business owner, Spa Director, College Principle to Corporate Director working in countries across Asia, Europe and the U.S.A.

Emma's wealth of knowledge, experience, fun and engaging personality coupled with her sheer passion for the industry makes her one of the most dynamic and eloquent speakers.

Title	International Speaker, Leading Industry Advocate and Director of Education at Dermalogica (APAC)
LinkedIn	Emma-Hobson
Instagram	Emma Hobson_IDI

Slowly silencing Henrietta

I will never forget my dad saying to me, "Emma, as you're not clever enough to go to university, you'll have to find something else to do for a living that does not include academia." Ironic, considering I now hold the role of Director of Education for the Asia Pacific...

I can't pin down the date nor any of the circumstances of our first meeting. Regardless, I do know she took up residence when I was a child. Her role has been to fill me with doubt, prevent me from taking risks and to make me think of playing small. She's grown and adapted over the years – sometimes a monster, sometimes a nagging voice in the rear. But always there, always making her presence felt.

Please allow me to introduce, Henrietta, my inner critic.

Henrietta is the name my dad wanted to call me. Thank goodness it was relegated down the order of options by my persuasive mum!

Henrietta and I have not been the best of friends since I was a child. Though I haven't managed to silence her completely, I am well on my way as she tires and becomes less vocal.

So, when does she like to appear and take over? A good example was recently when having lunch with an industry colleague I was meeting face to face for the first time. She is a woman I respect greatly for her accomplishments. The conversation started with her saying, "It's so exciting to finally meet you. You're such an industry icon and someone I have followed and respected throughout my career." Wow, that was quite a statement to be greeted with. Instead of glowing inside and being delighted to receive such kind, generous words, Henrietta said to me, "Ah… she's just trying to be kind. You really aren't that great and you certainly aren't deserving of such praise." In days of old, I would have let this internal dialogue have the better of me. But now after years of training, I know how to silence Henrietta and stop her rantings. As a result, I allowed myself to have a fabulous, positive, and thoroughly enjoyable meeting.

It is hard for some to accept praise and suppress their inner critic, especially if it's been deep seeded in their fabric since childhood. I have been working on how to slowly silence Henrietta for years. Today, I have her pretty much under control. It surprises me that she continues to try and make an appearance, often when I least expect, with the aim being to manipulate my self-belief and personal esteem.

Do you have a Henrietta living inside your head? I hope not, but sadly many of us do.

Self-doubt comes from many places, both distant and recent. I struggled at school with many subjects. Maths? Move along, nothing to see here. English? Hmm… maybe not. Too often I wondered if I lacked intelligence and vacillated between thinking yes and no.

We Yorkshire people are known for being direct and to the point, painfully so on occasion. My dad was a true-blue Yorkshireman and he made it clear that I needed to find a job not requiring a degree to attain it because I was "not university material." Based on my performance at the time, this assumption was probably correct.

Today, the reason I struggled at school would be glaringly obvious to any teacher. I'm dyslexic. It took a new graduate teacher who joined my school to recognise my learning difficulty just as I was about to leave. Sadly, this was a bit too late as Henrietta had got herself well and truly entrenched in my self-belief system by then.

The irony is that my father did steer me in the right direction toward a profession I could master and succeed in without needing to pander to my learning difficulties. The great thing about adversity is it allows you to develop your other skills. For me, it meant I had to rely on my ability to communicate and learn a trade utilising practical skills.

As fortune had it, I went into the booming business of health and wellness. Having been diagnosed with a learning difficulty made all the difference. At college, I studied my butt off to ensure I knew my stuff. I found tools to help me with my dyslexia. When it came to my finals, I managed much better with my written papers and excelled in my practical assessments. The final examination was conducted in front of a panel of four industry professionals, where I had a rigorous oral exam. Now I could finally prove I was not (entirely) stupid. The cherry on my cake was when my dad attended my graduation and it was announced I was to receive the top student of the year award, having achieved a 100 per cent pass rate and ranked the top of my year for the entire country. Praise was not part of his vocabulary, but I knew that inside he would have had an enormous sense of pride in my achievement. My very supportive mum, who was overseas at the time, was absolutely overjoyed.

So, at eighteen, I was ready to launch my career. But what did that look like? As one of my great loves was to travel, I decided to take a holiday in Hong Kong before finding myself a job. I loved this vibrant city. (How could I not, coming from a sleepy town in England?) A week into my holiday, I found myself sitting across from a very stern looking woman who was interviewing me for a role to establish a new business within their esteemed private Tennis Club. The position was to set up a spa from an empty shell and grow it to a thriving concern. Did I have the experience? Hell no! However, both my parents were business owners and I had worked in my mum's fashion business whilst at school and learnt a lot from her. Perhaps this was the reason I found myself in the interview saying, "Yes, I can do that. No problem." The great thing about being nineteen is you have the power of naivety. (The gift of the gab didn't hurt either!) Still, I was dumbfounded when my phone rang and the stern woman advised me I'd got the job.

Sadly, the bravado and confidence so apparent in my interview diminished quickly. Welcome back, Henrietta. Hello imposter syndrome. This was the perfect environment for Henrietta to take centre stage. I found myself working in a place where everyone was much older. All appeared to know what they were doing, except me. I now had two battles to fight.

- One was to ensure no one discovered I had no bloody clue what I was doing while pretending the opposite until I figured it out before getting found out.

- The second was listening to 'her', yes Henrietta, merrily chirping away in my head incessantly. She gloated while telling me I was out of my depth and was going to be fired.

If not for Maureen, the stern woman who interviewed me, Henrietta would have totally got the better of me and I would have given up, handed in my notice and scurried back home.

Maureen was my first mentor and an incredible boss. Even though I was riddled with self-doubt, (which I still can't quite fathom when I reflect on my eighteen-year-old self) Maureen believed in me. She saw something that made her feel I had the capability of doing the job well. Now that's what I call vision!

Nonetheless, let's say our relationship was not an instant hit! I first had to overcome being completely petrified every time I was in her presence. She was outwardly austere and always wore a cardigan no matter how hot it was. And believe me, Hong Kong gets very hot! When looking at me, she would lower her head slightly and gaze over the rim of her large, heavily magnified glasses perching on the end of her nose and give me a stern look. She reminded me of an old-fashioned, rather scary school principal. What gave her away was her beautiful, soft brown eyes behind those thick lenses. When I started to trust those eyes, I became more confident in her company. Then something remarkable happened... she began to warm to me in return. She offered guidance, and I, in turn, started to relax and listen. I quickly went about putting into practice her business and management advice. And it worked! As my trust in her grew, so did our relationship and her willingness to mentor me to become a proficient business manager and team leader.

by Emma Hobson

Maureen possessed many qualities and pearls of wisdom learnt over many years, including being in the secret service during the war. I imagine it would have been a very different world for her as an intelligent young woman wanting to get ahead. Not that I appreciated that at my tender age.

When I doubted my ability to make decisions, she did not make them for me even though that would have been easy for her to do. Instead, she would simply say, "Emma, think through the issues. Consider the consequences and the effects your decision may have positively or negatively on your team and the business. Once done, make the decision. You must learn to trust yourself when making decisions and be accountable for them. If you still have doubts after this process, ask yourself what your gut tells you to do. Learn to trust that you have the answers. Second-guessing yourself won't help. If it turns out to be the wrong one, it's okay because this is how you learn. You won't get it right all of the time."

Those two and a half years in the role gave me the best foundation I could have ever hoped for and one that allowed me to build my career and leadership skills. I am forever grateful to Maureen, a sagacious and generous woman, my very first professional mentor.

The story of success is different for everyone. In this book, you will find so many words of wisdom from some incredible women. Again, I have had to silence Henrietta, who has told me, "You don't deserve to be in this book because your story can't be as meaningful or as valuable to the reader as everyone else's." All I can hope for is that you disagree with her.

One of the critical things I attribute to my career success is acquiring knowledge. This has become an integral part of my life. I know I can learn so much if I choose to have my antenna up and tune in to the right signals. This ensures I put myself in the space where I can learn the most.

One way I learned to control Henrietta was to read countless books and listen to audio recordings on self-empowerment. There are numerous exercises the experts share. Some resonate. Some do not. One author suggests standing in front of a mirror morning and evening and looking yourself in the eye and saying over and over and over again 'I like myself, I like myself, I like myself" until you get so comfortable with yourself you actually believe it. It sounds like a simple exercise but it was much harder than I imagined. It took months before I could say those words, look myself in the eye and feel I was speaking my truth. It's an exercise I've had to revisit when my self-worth has been compromised.

Why is it women have such low opinions of themselves? Is it because we pick up messages from childhood, both subliminally and directly, that we are just not quite perfect? Too fat, too short, too opinionated, too stupid. You know the list.

So, what should we be listening to and are we listening to it?

It is apparent to me the act of listening seems to be underrated and underutilised. It seems people don't have the time to listen, only sufficient time to speak. I would not be where I am if I had spoken more than I had listened. Listening intently and being present allows me to always have a deeper understanding of the message's context and content and to analyse if it is positive and has value.

I remember attending a presentation given by Anita Roderick (Founder of the Body Shop) and came away feeling I had electricity running through my veins. I was so inspired by her words and her vision. Another such woman is Jane Wurwand, Founder and Visionary of Dermalogica. When Jane speaks, people feel compelled to listen. She is a woman of great foresight, sharing her insights into human behaviour as well as her astute business intellect.

When I first tuned in to Jane, I wanted to be just like her. For a time, I tried to copy the way she delivered a presentation. However, I never nailed it. Why? Because I am not Jane Wurwand. I am Emma Hobson. What time and self-worth taught me is if people are going to listen to what I had to say as a speaker, I had to share my own message. I needed to use my words and experiences to show my personality and learn to be vulnerable and authentic with an audience. Of course, I can quote great women such as Jane, share some of their wisdom, but I have to say it using my voice.

It seems strange so many of us struggle with just being our authentic selves. We don't trust that people will like the real us because we feel our authentic self is not good enough for others to appreciate. Ever wondered where your inner critic comes from? This could be the place.

So what has all this work on myself led to? To trust and believe in my capabilities. This allows me to nurture the self-belief and worth of others. In turn, I enable them to be the best version of themselves, ensuring they have no need to suffer from imposter syndrome. I seek to empower them in believing they can succeed with their projects, trust their capabilities and not fear failure as this is inevitable if you want to be innovative and progressive. They need me to believe in them and provide opportunities to grow and move up. And sometimes, they may need to move on. Does this style of management sound familiar? Was this not the lesson I learnt so long ago when working for Maureen? Her mentorship has served me well all my life. I aspire to do for those that come under my guardianship what Maureen did for me.

In knowledge acquisition, I have also learnt that caring for people and making them feel valued requires you to be present with them, check-in and listen to what they have to say. It makes you listen to where they are – their frustrations, roadblocks, aspirations. This means you need to ask the right questions and, yes, practice that all-important skill of listening intently to their answers. You must check into their internal barometer and learn how they measure themselves. For when I have a true understanding of this, I know where my work must lie.

If you are a leader, especially in a medium to large corporation, you also need to be acutely aware that the profit mill should never become the key driver for your team. It is a given their actions and contribution will result in financial success. My team are aware of our numbers and our objectives. However, what drives people is a purpose, not profit. If I do not lead with purpose and provide them continually with the 'why' they will not have the reason to want to succeed. This is where I believe, as women, we excel in leadership; our emotional intelligence connects people with purpose. Human beings are naturally inquisitive. Anyone who has had a conversation with a four-year-old child knows "But why?" is the most dominant thought and must be answered a million times a day.

Successfully connecting your people to your purpose is where loyalty and longevity reside. Not only have I by Emma Hobson

worked for the same company for twenty-seven years, but there are plenty on my team who've had their fifteen and twenty-year anniversaries too. Our loyalty is bonded to our purpose. We are each empowered to think for ourselves and make our own decisions. Skills are developed and stretched as innovation constantly challenges us to be the best version of ourselves. We work in a team centred around trust and respect, and just like a sports team, if we have a player down, we all rally together with a network of support. This type of team culture can only occur when self-doubt is replaced by self-worth.

This brings me to my last words around mentorship. I know some amazingly talented, incredibly successful people who have so much wisdom, incredible leadership skills and business acumen to share. Yet, they are hardly ever approached to be mentors. Why don't women like to ask others for such guidance and support? Perhaps the answer lies with that dammed voice in our head telling us we really aren't good enough or deserving of their help.

Well, it's time to silence that inner critic. If I have managed to overcome the challenges of my dyslexia, look myself in a mirror without judgment and tell Henrietta to "Shut the **** up!" then so can you.

www.ingramcontent.com/pod-product-compliance
Lightning Source LLC
Chambersburg PA
CBHW052013030426

42334CB00029BA/3201